DO ONE

THING
EVERY DAY

This

AWESOME

journal belongs to:

_____

JUST DON'T EXPECT ME TO BE ALL "DEAR DIARY" THIS AND "DEAR DIARY" THAT.

Jeff Kinney, Diary of a Wimpy Kid

▲
▼

DO YOU WRITE in a journal at school? Do you keep a writer's notebook? Did your mom give you a diary? Enough is enough, right? Wrong!

This is a different kind of journal. You can write or draw. You can turn to whichever page in whatever order you want. You can go forward or backward from day to day depending on your mood. Does a quotation from *Wonder* or Harry Potter or Dork Diaries catch your eye, or a silly poem called "The Goops"? The words of a famous inventor (Thomas Edison) or athlete (Chloe Kim), or a Roman poet you've never heard of (Ovid)? If so, read on and write or draw your response.

Special features also loop through the pages. Do you feel like listing your favorite shows? Look for a "Top 5." You can imagine a future technology ("I Predict") or describe how you would use a superpower ("*IF . . . IF . . . IF . . .*"). You can "See Things Differently" by changing a paper clip into a surfboard or a doodle into an animal. If you want to help someone else, choose a "Lend a Hand" page. You can "Write Something Weird" or "Draw Something Weird."

Best of all, this book is yours alone. No one will correct it or give it a grade. No points marked off for misspelled words. In fact, you will be the one to do the grading. Begin by rating your life on the "Awesome Meter" on this page, and end with the "Awesome Meter" on the very last page. In between, you will get to think about some things you never thought about before, and learn more about yourself without even trying—have fun!

This is how I rate my life right now:

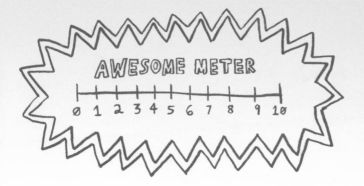

The family is one of nature's masterpieces.

George Santayana

Fill in the names on your family tree.

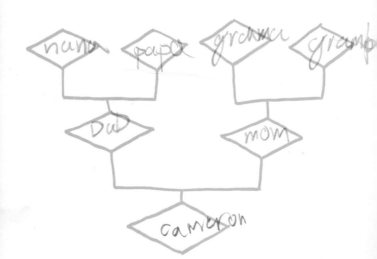

Draw a portrait of your family, starring you.

I AM FOND OF PIGS. DOGS
DOWN ON US. PIGS TREAT

DATE: __ / __ / __

Not to brag or anything, but I am kind of a big deal to my:

○ dog

○ cat

○ pig

○ goldfish

○ bird

○ other: _____

OOK UP TO US. CATS LOOK
JS AS EQUALS. ◀ Winston Churchill

DATE: __ / __ / __

Draw your adoring pet or a pet you would adore.

DATE: __ / __ / __

Sleep is when all the unsorted stuff comes flying out as from a dustbin upset in a high wind.

William Golding, *Pincher Martin*

Stuff that came flying out in my dream last night:

_____

_____

_____

_____

_____

_____

THE NEXT DAY, WHEN I GOT UP, FUDGE'S BED WAS EMPTY. HE DOESN'T KNOW YOU'RE SUPPOSED TO SLEEP LATE WHEN YOU'RE ON VACATION.

Judy Blume, *Fudge-a-Mania*

Today is a vacation day. The clock looked like this when I got out of bed:

○ A.M.
○ P.M.

When you hug someone, you learn something else about them. An important something else.

E. L. Konigsburg,
From the Mixed-Up Files of Mrs. Basil E. Frankweiler

The best hug I got today:

_____

_____

_____

_____

_____

LOVE IS SHARING YOUR POPCORN.

Charles M. Schulz, *Peanuts*

I think love is sharing your _____.

Lend a Hand

Collect the toys and games in your room that are too babyish for you now. Clean them off and give them to kids in a shelter or daycare program or to a younger kid you know.

◯ Did it today!

IF YOU THINK YOU ARE TOO SMALL TO MAKE A DIFFERENCE, TRY SLEEPING WITH A MOSQUITO.

Dalai Lama

Something small I did today that made a difference:

- ◯ smiled at a new teacher
- ◯ talked to a new classmate
- ◯ called my grandparents
- ◯ taught a little kid how to play a game
- ◯ completed someone else's chore—surprise!
- ◯ other: _____

u should go eat
a waffle!
u can't be sad if u eat
a waffle!!!

Lauren Myracle, ttfn

Draw a picture of your go-to comfort food.

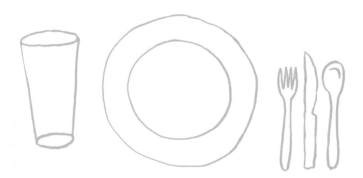

I'M PRESIDENT OF THE UNITED STATES, AND I'M NOT GOING TO EAT ANY MORE BROCCOLI!

George H. W. Bush

When I'm president of the United States, I'm not going to eat any

more _____!

DATE: __ / __ / __

MY TOP 5 MOVIES/SHOWS

1 _____

2 _____

3 _____

4 _____

5 _____

Today I saw _____.

A long time ago in a galaxy far, far away . . .

▲
George Lucas, *Star Wars*
▼

Write the opening setup for the next episode of *Star Wars* or a movie based on your favorite book or your own original idea.

_____

_____

_____

_____

_____

_____

DO THE SCARY THING FIRST, AND GET SCARED LATER.

Lemony Snicket, *When Did You See Her Last?*

DATE: __ / __ / __

I DID THIS SUPER-SCARY THING TODAY:

_____

_____

DATE: __ / __ / __

DRAW THE WORLD'S SCARIEST ROLLER COASTER.

I predict I will be a _____ when I grow up.

What is the point of being alive if you don't at least try to do something remarkable?

John Green, *An Abundance of Katherines*

I am going to try to do this remarkable thing today:

_____

_____

_____

_____

_____

These are some awesome people I know:

DATE: __ / __ / __

These are some awesome people I don't know (but wish I did!):

The only
certainty
is that
nothing
is certain.

Pliny the Elder

DATE: __ / __ / __

I WAS SURE THIS WOULD HAPPEN TODAY—BUT IT DIDN'T:

_____

_____

_____

_____

_____

DATE: __ / __ / __

I WAS SURE THIS WOULDN'T HAPPEN TODAY—BUT IT DID:

_____

_____

_____

_____

_____

I AM THANKFUL FOR LAUGHTER, EXCEPT WHEN MILK COMES OUT OF MY NOSE.

Woody Allen

Draw yourself laughing so hard that milk is coming out of your nose.

DATE: __ / __ / __

THE WORST WASTED OF ALL DAYS IS THAT DURING WHICH ONE HAS NOT LAUGHED.

Sébastien R. N. Chamfort

What cracked me up today:

_____

_____

_____

_____

_____

_____

_____

SEE THINGS

Turn these paperclips into a surfboard, a snowshoe, a loaf of bread, a mummy, or something else!

DIFFERENTLY

DATE: __ / __ / __

Turn this doodle into an animal (real or imaginary). Label it.

TOTO, I HAVE A FEELING WE'RE NOT IN KANSAS ANYMORE.

Dorothy, in *The Wizard of Oz*

Something crazy at a place I visited today:

_____

_____

_____

_____

_____

I had ants in Africa recently: they were rather nice and crispy.

Desmond Morris

Something gross I ate today:

_____

_____

_____

_____

_____

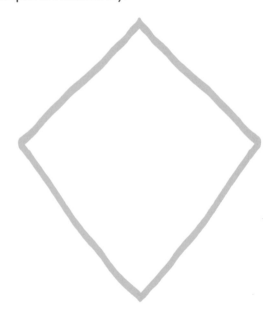

FILLING A SPACE IN
THAT'S WHAT AR

DATE: __ / __ / __

Fill this space in a beautiful way:

A BEAUTIFUL WAY.
MEANS TO ME. ◀ Georgia O'Keeffe

DATE: __ / __ / __

Fill this space in a beautiful way:

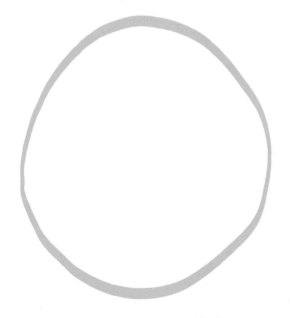

ALL FOR ONE, ONE FOR ALL.

Alexandre Dumas, *The Three Musketeers*

My crew:

_____

_____

_____

_____

_____

It is not often that someone comes along who is a true friend and a good writer.

E. B. White, *Charlotte's Web*

A note from a friend that made me smile today:

_____

_____

_____

_____

_____

SNORING KEEPS THE MONSTERS AWAY.

Judy Blume, *Fudge-a-Mania*

How I scare monsters away:

_____

_____

_____

_____

Place yourself in the monster's mouth.

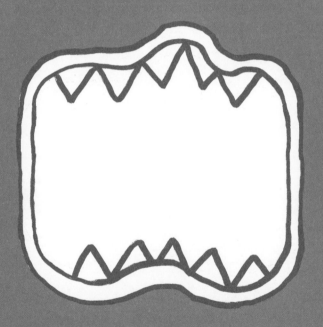

I CAN LIVE
FOR TWO
MONTHS ON
A GOOD
COMPLIMENT.

Mark Twain

DATE: __ / __ / __

I GOT THIS COMPLIMENT TODAY:

_____

_____

_____

_____

_____

DATE: __ / __ / __

I GAVE THIS COMPLIMENT TO _____ TODAY:

_____

_____

_____

_____

_____

Now he couldn't stop
thinking about that honey.
It would be worth a sting
or two just to have
a taste of it.

Elizabeth George Speare, *The Sign of the Beaver*

A treat I worked hard to get today:

_____

_____

_____

_____

DATE: __ / __ / __

A CUCUMBER SHOULD BE WELL SLICED, AND DRESSED WITH PEPPER AND VINEGAR, AND THEN THROWN OUT, AS GOOD FOR NOTHING.

Samuel Johnson

These foods should be thrown out as good for nothing:

_____

_____

_____

_____

_____

DATE: __ / __ / __

IF I COULD LIVE ANYWHERE IN THE WORLD,
THIS IS WHERE IT WOULD BE:

_____

_____

WHY?

_____

_____

_____

_____

IF...

DATE: __ / __ / __

IF I COULD LIVE ANYWHERE IMAGINARY,
THIS IS WHERE IT WOULD BE:

_____

_____

WHY?

_____

_____

_____

_____

DATE: __ / __ / __

IT HAS BEEN A TERRIBLE, HORRIBLE, NO GOOD, VERY BAD DAY. MY MOM SAYS SOME DAYS ARE LIKE THAT. EVEN IN AUSTRALIA.

Judith Viorst,
Alexander and the Terrible, Horrible, No Good, Very Bad Day

Why today was a terrible, horrible, no good, very bad day:

_____

_____

_____

_____

DATE: __ / __ / __

[I] WISH THAT LIFE HAD A FAST FORWARD BUTTON.

Dan Chopin

I wish I could fast-forward past this event today:

_____

_____

_____

_____

I am not plain or
average or—
god forbid—vanilla.
I am peanut butter
rocky road with
multicolored sprinkles,
hot fudge, and a cherry
on top.

Wendy Mass, *Every Soul a Star*

DRAW YOURSELF AS AN ICE CREAM CONCOCTION.

DESCRIBE YOUR ICE CREAM CONCOCTION.

_____

_____

_____

I HAVE SELDOM HEARD A TRAIN GO BY AND NOT WISHED I WAS ON IT.

Paul Theroux, *The Great Railway Bazaar*

I wish I was going on a train to _____ today.

DATE: __ / __ / __

THERE IS NO PLACE LIKE HOME.

L. Frank Baum, *The Wonderful Wizard of Oz*

Why I liked staying home today:

_____

_____

_____

_____

MY TOP 5 BOOKS

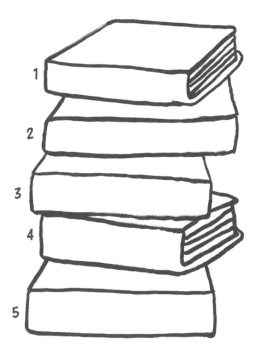

1

2

3

4

5

Now I am reading _____.

A good book is the best of friends, the same today and for ever.

Martin Farquhar Tupper, "Of Reading"

The book that is my BFF:

_____

_____

_____

_____

Decorate these shoes and socks for school.

Decorate these shoes and socks for a party.

THE GREAT PLEASURE IN LIFE IS DOING WHAT PEOPLE SAY YOU CANNOT DO.

Walter Bagehot

DATE: __ / __ / __

PEOPLE SAY THAT I CANNOT DO THIS:

_____

_____

_____

_____

_____

DATE: __ / __ / __

TODAY I DID THE IMPOSSIBLE:

_____

_____

_____

_____

_____

What is a family, after all, except memories?

Joyce Carol Oates, *We Were the Mulvaneys*

My craziest family memory:

_____

_____

_____

_____

_____

FAMILY JOKES . . .
ARE THE BOND THAT KEEPS
MOST FAMILIES ALIVE.

Stella Benson

My favorite family joke:

_____

_____

_____

_____

_____

WRITE SOMETHING WEIRD

Write something weird about your toilet.

_____

_____

_____

_____

_____

_____

_____

_____

_____

_____

DRAW SOMETHING WEIRD

Draw something weird coming out of your toilet.

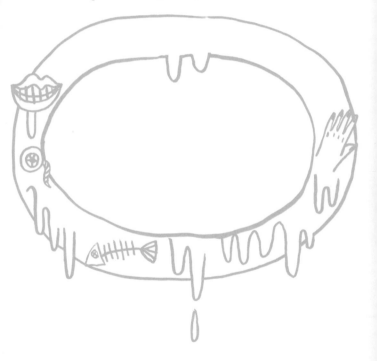

THE MORE HE GAVE AWAY, THE MORE DELIGHTED HE BECAME.

Marcus Pfister, *The Rainbow Fish*

I was delighted to give all these things away:

_____

_____

_____

_____

_____

They gave it me— for an un-birthday present.

Lewis Carroll, *Through the Looking Glass*

Hooray! I got this un-birthday present today:

_____

_____

_____

_____

_____

TO LIKE AND DISLIKE THE SAME THINGS, THAT IS INDEED TRUE FRIENDSHIP.

Sallust

DATE: __ / __ / __

WHAT MY FRIENDS AND I ALL LIKE:

_____

_____

_____

_____

DATE: __ / __ / __

WHAT MY FRIENDS AND I ALL DISLIKE:

_____

_____

_____

_____

I HAVE SO MUCH TO DO THAT I AM GOING TO BED.

Savoyard proverb

What I put off doing today:

_____

_____

_____

_____

_____

DATE: __ / __ / __

LYING IN BED WOULD BE AN ALTOGETHER PERFECT AND SUPREME EXPERIENCE IF ONLY ONE HAD A COLORED PENCIL LONG ENOUGH TO DRAW ON THE CEILING.

G. K. Chesterton, "On Lying in Bed"

Lying in bed today would be perfect for me if only:

_____

_____

_____

_____

I NEVER SAID, "I WANT TO BE ALONE." . . . I ONLY SAID, "I WANT TO BE *LET* ALONE."

Greta Garbo

When I like to be *let* alone:

_____

_____

_____

I am on my mountain in a tree home that people have passed without ever knowing that I am here.

Jean Craighead George, *My Side of the Mountain*

Where I went to be alone today:

_____

_____

_____

NOBODY CARES IF YOU CAN'T DANCE WELL. JUST GET UP AND DANCE.

Dave Barry

I ◯ can ◯ can't dance well.

Where I just got up and danced today:

_____

_____

_____

My Dance Playlist

COLIN IS THE SORT OF NAME YOU GIVE YOUR GOLDFISH FOR A JOKE.

Colin Firth

DATE: __ / __ / __

MY FAVORITE GIRL'S NAME:

DATE: __ / __ / __

MY FAVORITE BOY'S NAME:

DATE: __ / __ / __

Nothing great was ever achieved without enthusiasm.

Ralph Waldo Emerson

What I achieved today with enthusiasm:

_____

_____

_____

_____

_____

DATE: __ / __ / __

NEVER DO ANYTHING BY HALVES
IF YOU WANT TO GET AWAY WITH IT.
BE OUTRAGEOUS. GO THE WHOLE HOG.
MAKE SURE EVERYTHING YOU DO IS SO
COMPLETELY CRAZY IT'S UNBELIEVABLE.

Roald Dahl, *Matilda*

I did this crazy outrageous thing today:

_____

_____

_____

_____

_____

MANY'S THE LONG NIGHT I'VE DREAMED OF CHEESE— TOASTED, MOSTLY.

Robert Louis Stevenson, *Treasure Island*

A food I dreamed about:

_____

PARSLEY
IS GHARSLEY.

Ogden Nash, "Further Reflections on Parsley"

I think _____ is gharsley.

DATE: __ / __ / __

Copy this coupon for tech support
and give it to someone who needs help:

○ Did it today!

DATE: ___ / ___ / ___

Three things in human life are
important. The first is to be
kind. The second is to be kind.
And the third is to be kind.

Henry James

Something kind I did today:

_____

_____

_____

_____

DATE: __ / __ / __

ONE DAY'S EXPOSURE TO MOUNTAINS IS BETTER THAN CARTLOADS OF BOOKS.

John Muir

What I learned from being in nature today:

_____

_____

_____

_____

_____

DATE: __ / __ / __

MRS. JEWLS SAID THAT A LOT OF PEOPLE LEARN BEST WHEN THEY STARE OUT A WINDOW.

Louis Sachar, *Sideways Stories from Wayside School*

What I learned staring out the classroom window today:

_____

_____

_____

_____

_____

MY TOP 5 OUTFITS

Today I wore _____.

Happiness and confidence are the prettiest things you can wear.

Taylor Swift

Today I wore happiness and confidence to

_____.

A PLACE FOR EVERYTHING AND EVERYTHING IN ITS PLACE.

Isabella Beeton, The Book of Household Management

DATE: __ / __ / __

DRAW YOUR ROOM HERE:

DATE: __ / __ / __

HOW I WOULD DESCRIBE MY ROOM: ○ spotless

○ everything in its place

○ neat

○ lived-in

○ messy

○ a pigsty

○ a national disaster area

○ other: _____

*And so for a time it looked
as if all the adventures
were coming to an end;
but that was not to be.*

C. S. Lewis, *The Lion, the Witch, and the Wardrobe*

An adventure I had today:

_____

_____

_____

_____

_____

DATE: __ / __ / __

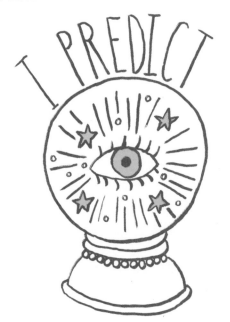

I predict that my greatest adventure ever will be:

_____

_____

_____

DATE: __ / __ / __

Draw a self-portrait with your right hand here:

DATE: __ / __ / __

Draw a self-portrait with your left hand here:

THE GOOPS ARE
GLUTTONOUS
AND RUDE,
THEY GUG AND
GUMBLE WITH
THEIR FOOD.

Gelett Burgess, *Goops and How to Be Them*

DATE: __ / __ / __

MY GOOP-Y EATING HABITS:

_____

_____

_____

_____

_____

DATE: __ / __ / __

THE MOST DISGUSTING GOOP-Y EATING HABITS IN MY FAMILY:

_____

_____

_____

_____

_____

MOST OF THE BASIC MATERIAL A WRITER WORKS WITH IS ACQUIRED BEFORE THE AGE OF FIFTEEN.

Willa Cather

A great story I will save for when I am writing a book:

_____

_____

_____

_____

_____

The world is full of talkers, but it
is rare to find anyone who listens.
And I assure you that you can pick
up more information when you are
listening than when you are talking.

E. B. White, *The Trumpet of the Swan*

Information I picked up by listening today:

_____

_____

_____

_____

_____

SEE THINGS

Turn these pencil shavings into a hat, a lampshade, a roof, a fat pencil, or something else!

DIFFERENTLY

DATE: __ / __ / __

Turn this doodle into a person (real or imaginary). Label it.

"WILL POWER IS TRYING HARD
NOT TO DO SOMETHING THAT YOU
REALLY WANT TO DO," SAID FROG.
"YOU MEAN LIKE TRYING *NOT* TO
EAT ALL OF THESE COOKIES?"
ASKED TOAD.

Arnold Lobel, *Frog and Toad Together*

Draw a plate of cookies it would take willpower for you not to eat.

TO PROMISE NOT TO DO A THING IS THE SUREST WAY IN THE WORLD TO MAKE A BODY WANT TO GO AND DO THAT VERY THING.

Mark Twain, *The Adventures of Tom Sawyer*

The very thing I want to do today (though I promised not to):

_____

_____

_____

_____

_____

I don't really like knees.

Yves Saint Laurent

DATE: __ / __ / __

I *don't* really like:

◯ toes

◯ eyebrows

◯ freckles

◯ elbows

◯ ears

◯ knees

DATE: __ / __ / __

I *do* really like:

◯ toes

◯ eyebrows

◯ freckles

◯ elbows

◯ ears

◯ knees

LET OTHERS PRAISE ANCIENT TIMES; I AM GLAD I WAS BORN IN THESE.

Ovid

Why I am glad to be living now:

_____

_____

_____

_____

_____

DATE: __ / __ / __

My favorite thing is to go where I've never been.

Diane Arbus

Check off where you want to go that you've never been:

○ Antarctica

○ Africa

○ the North Pole

○ the moon

○ Mount Everest

○ other: _____

DATE: __ / __ / __

IT'S CRAZY!
BUT I DO FEEL MORE
CONFIDENT WHEN
I HAVE SHORT HAIR.

Millie Bobby Brown

I feel more _____

when I have _____ hair.

Draw your hair on a Good Hair Day and a Bad Hair Day.

FRIENDS SHARE ALL THINGS.

Pythagoras

DATE: __ / __ / __

SOMETHING I SHARED WITH A FRIEND TODAY:

_____

_____

_____

_____

_____

DATE: __ / __ / __

SOMETHING A FRIEND SHARED WITH ME TODAY:

_____

_____

_____

_____

_____

NOW, WHAT I WANT IS, FACTS. . . . FACTS ALONE ARE WANTED IN LIFE.

Charles Dickens, *Hard Times*

A cool fact I learned today:

_____

_____

_____

_____

_____

DON'T TRY TO COMPREHEND WITH YOUR MIND. YOUR MINDS ARE VERY LIMITED. USE YOUR INTUITION.

Madeleine L'Engle, *A Wind in the Door*

How I used my intuition today:

_____

_____

_____

_____

_____

DATE: __ / __ / __

IF I WON A MILLION DOLLARS, THIS IS HOW I WOULD SPEND IT ON MYSELF:

_____

_____

_____

_____

_____

_____

_____

_____

 **IF...**

DATE: __/__/__

IF I WON A MILLION DOLLARS, THIS IS HOW I WOULD SPEND IT ON OTHERS:

_____

_____

_____

_____

_____

_____

_____

_____

FROM THIS DAY ON AND FOREVER, I WILL NEVER USE THE WORD **PEN** AGAIN. INSTEAD, I WILL USE THE WORD **FRINDLE,** AND I WILL DO EVERYTHING POSSIBLE SO OTHERS WILL, TOO.

Andrew Clements, *Frindle*

From this day on and forever, I will never use the word _____

again. Instead, I will use the word _____.

THE ONLY STUPID THING ABOUT WORDS IS THE SPELLING OF THEM.

Laura Ingalls Wilder

Circle the correct spellings of these commonly misspelled words:

abot	about	aboat
separet	separite	separate
believe	beleive	blieve
thuoght	thought	thoght
difrent	differint	different

I THINK I CAN.
I THINK I CAN.
I THINK I CAN . . .
I THOUGHT I COULD.
I THOUGHT I COULD.
I THOUGHT I COULD.

Watty Piper, *The Little Engine That Could*

DATE: __ / __ / __

I THINK I CAN:

_____

_____

_____

_____

_____

DATE: __ / __ / __

I THOUGHT I COULD:

_____

_____

_____

_____

_____

DATE: __ / __ / __

THE END OF THE WORLD STARTED WHEN A PEGASUS LANDED ON THE HOOD OF MY CAR.

Rick Riordan, *The Last Olympian*

Something terrible that happened today:

_____

_____

_____

_____

_____

Fall down seven times, get up eight.

Japanese proverb

How I got up after something bad happened to me today:

_____

_____

_____

_____

_____

DATE: __/__/__

MY TOP 5 SONGS

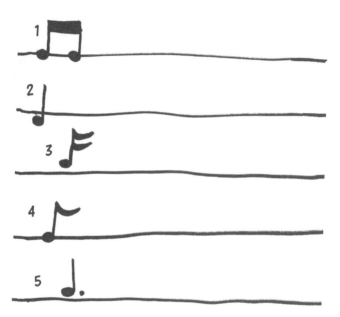

Today I listened to _____.

PHOTO

STARRING ME!

Selfie shot at arm's length:

Close-up of my pet:

My head seen from above:

"We all can dance,"
he said, "when we find
music that we love."

Giles Andreae, *Giraffes Can't Dance*

Music that makes me want to dance:

_____

_____

_____

_____

_____

GALLERY

DATE: __ / __ / __

SUPPORTING CAST!

Family member sleeping:

My BFF upside down:

Photobomb:

EVERYONE IN
THE WORLD
SHOULD GET
A STANDING
OVATION AT
LEAST ONCE IN
THEIR LIVES.

R. J. Palacio, *Wonder*

DATE: __ / __ / __

WHY I GOT A STANDING OVATION TODAY:

_____

_____

_____

_____

_____

DATE: __ / __ / __

WHY I GAVE A STANDING OVATION TODAY:

_____

_____

_____

_____

_____

DATE: __ / __ / __

I PUT A PIECE OF PAPER AND A PENCIL UNDER MY PILLOW, AND WHEN I COULD NOT SLEEP I WROTE IN THE DARK.

Henry David Thoreau

What I did when I couldn't sleep last night:

_____

_____

_____

_____

_____

YOU CAN ONLY LEARN TO BE A BETTER WRITER BY ACTUALLY WRITING.

Doris Lessing

I learned to be a better _____

by actually _____.

WRITE SOMETHING WEIRD

Write about something weird that happened or might happen at your school.

_____

_____

_____

_____

_____

_____

_____

_____

_____

_____

DRAW SOMETHING WEIRD

Draw a picture of something weird in the playground.

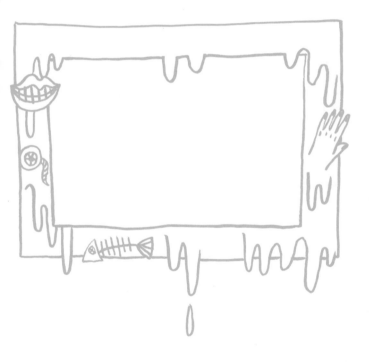

DATE: __ / __ / __

YOU'RE NEVER TOO OLD TO DO GOOFY STUFF.

Ward Cleaver, in *Leave It to Beaver*

Goofy stuff I did today:

_____

_____

_____

_____

_____

Nonsense wakes up the brain cells.

Dr. Seuss

Some nonsense that woke up my brain cells today:

_____

_____

_____

_____

_____

WHAT REALLY KNOCKS ME OUT IS A BOOK THAT, WHEN YOU'RE ALL DONE READING IT, YOU WISH THE AUTHOR THAT WROTE IT WAS A TERRIFIC FRIEND OF YOURS AND YOU COULD CALL HIM UP ON THE PHONE WHENEVER YOU FELT LIKE IT.

J. D. Salinger, *The Catcher in the Rye*

DATE: __ / __ / __

AUTHORS WHOSE PHONE NUMBERS I WOULD LOVE TO HAVE:

_____

_____

_____

_____

_____

DATE: __ / __ / __

WHAT I WOULD SAY TO MY FAVORITE AUTHOR, _____:

_____

_____

_____

_____

_____

DATE: __ / __ / __

I HAD ALWAYS THOUGHT THAT ONCE YOU GREW UP YOU COULD DO ANYTHING YOU WANTED—STAY UP ALL NIGHT OR EAT ICE-CREAM STRAIGHT OUT OF THE CONTAINER.

Bill Bryson, *The Lost Continent*

What I want to do once I grow up:

_____

_____

_____

_____

_____

It's no use going back
to yesterday, because
I was a different
person then.

Lewis Carroll, *Alice's Adventures in Wonderland*

How I am different now from how I was yesterday:

_____

_____

_____

_____

_____

Oh, it's delightful to have
ambitions. I'm so glad I have
such a lot. . . . Just as soon as
you attain to one ambition
you see another one glittering
higher up still.

L. M. Montgomery, *Anne of Green Gables*

My latest ambition:

_____

_____

_____

_____

FANCY BEING REMEMBERED AROUND THE WORLD FOR THE INVENTION OF A MOUSE!

Walt Disney

What I want to be remembered for:

_____

_____

_____

_____

_____

Nothing says holidays like a cheese log.

Ellen DeGeneres

Nothing says my birthday like _____.

Nothing says Thanksgiving like _____.

Nothing says _____ like _____.

DATE: __ / __ / __

Create your own holidays:

National Love Your _____ Day, date: __ / __ / __
(noun)

National _____ Day, date: __ / __ / __
(color)

National _____ Day, date: __ / __ / __
(game)

National _____ Day, date: __ / __ / __
(insect)

National _____ Day, date: __ / __ / __
(junk food)

National _____ Day, date: __ / __ / __
(something else)

½ THE TROUBLE IN THIS WORLD IS CAUSED BY SAYING YES TOO QUICK AND THE OTHER ½ BY NOT SAYING NO QUICKER.

Josh Billings, *Josh Billings' Wit and Humor*

DATE: __ / __ / __

I SAID YES TO THIS TOO QUICK TODAY:

_____

_____

_____

_____

_____

DATE: __ / __ / __

I DIDN'T SAY NO TO THIS QUICK ENOUGH TODAY:

_____

_____

_____

_____

_____

I'LL GIVE YOU A DEFINITE MAYBE.

Sam Goldwyn

I made this big decision today about _____:

○ yes

○ no

○ maybe

DATE: __ / __ / __

YOU MUST NEVER FEEL BADLY ABOUT
MAKING MISTAKES . . . AS LONG AS YOU TAKE
THE TROUBLE TO LEARN FROM THEM. FOR YOU
OFTEN LEARN MORE BY BEING WRONG FOR
THE RIGHT REASONS THAN YOU DO BY BEING
RIGHT FOR THE WRONG REASONS.

Norton Juster, *The Phantom Tollbooth*

What I learned from being wrong today:

_____

_____

_____

_____

He only does it to annoy, Because he knows it teases.

Lewis Carroll, *Alice's Adventures in Wonderland*

How someone at school was annoying today:

_____

_____

_____

_____

_____

"I am **not** a pest," Ramona Quimby told her big sister Beezus.

Beverly Cleary, *Ramona the Pest*

How someone in my family was a pest today:

_____

_____

_____

_____

_____

Lend a Hand

Adopt a nearby tree by checking on it once a week. Water it when the soil is dry. Wearing gloves, pick up litter around its base.

○ Did it today!

DATE: __ / __ / __

UNLESS SOMEONE LIKE YOU CARES A WHOLE AWFUL LOT, NOTHING IS GOING TO GET BETTER. IT'S NOT.

Dr. Seuss, *The Lorax*

How I helped the environment today:

_____

_____

_____

_____

_____

CURIOUSLY ENOUGH, ONE CANNOT READ A BOOK: ONE CAN ONLY REREAD IT.

Vladimir Nabokov

A book I love to read again and again:

_____

_____

_____

_____

READING CAN BE A ROAD TO FREEDOM OR A KEY TO A SECRET GARDEN, WHICH, IF TENDED, WILL TRANSFORM ALL OF LIFE.

Katherine Paterson

How reading transformed my life today:

_____

_____

_____

_____

MY TOP 5 OUTDOOR ACTIVITIES

Today I _____.

To me, teamwork is the beauty of our sport, where you have five acting as one.

Mike Krzyzewski

What I contributed to my team today:

_____

_____

_____

_____

_____

Ideas won't keep. Something must be done about them.

Alfred North Whitehead

DATE: __ / __ / __

A GREAT IDEA I HAD TODAY:

_____

_____

_____

_____

_____

DATE: __ / __ / __

HOW I CAN MAKE MY GREAT IDEA A REALITY:

_____

_____

_____

_____

_____

I predict that when I grow up, people will be wearing

_____ .

FASHION
IS MADE
TO BECOME
UNFASHIONABLE.

Coco Chanel

I used to think _____ was fashionable.

Now I think it is _____.

Write your signature in different styles here:

BUBBLE

chalk

digital

ROBOT

Old-fashioned

DATE: __ / __ / __

Combine your initials into a monogram for your backpack here:

IT WAS ALL BECAUSE OF [MY] NO-GOOD-DIRTY-ROTTEN-PIG-STEALING-GREAT-GREAT-GRANDFATHER.

Louis Sachar, *Holes*

DATE: __ / __ / __

EXCUSE I GAVE TO MY PARENTS TODAY FOR _____:

_____

_____

_____

_____

_____

DATE: __ / __ / __

EXCUSE I GAVE TO MY TEACHER TODAY FOR _____:

_____

_____

_____

_____

_____

DATE: __ / __ / __

There was only orange juice in the fridge. Nothing else that you could put on cereal, unless you think that ketchup or mayonnaise or pickle juice would be nice on your Toastios, which I do not.

Neil Gaiman, *Fortunately, the Milk*

What I made for a snack when the fridge was basically empty:

_____

_____

_____

_____

_____

*Rice is great
if you're really hungry
and want to eat two
thousand of something.*

Mitch Hedberg

What I go for when I am really hungry:

_____

_____

_____

_____

_____

SEE THINGS

DATE: __ / __ / __

Turn these rubber bands into a bird's nest, curly hair, a fuzzy animal, a fancy necklace, or something else!

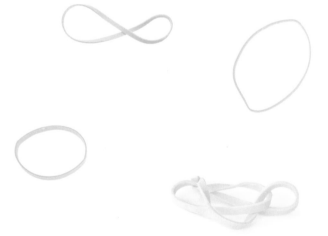

DIFFERENTLY

DATE: __ / __ / __

Turn this doodle into a food (real or imaginary). Label it.

DATE: __ / __ / __

NO DUTY IS MORE URGENT THAN THAT OF RETURNING THANKS.

Saint Ambrose

Today I thanked _____ for the

Best. Gift. Ever: _____.

A polite thank-you note I wrote for something I didn't want in the first place:

NOW A PENGUIN MAY LOO
ROOM, BUT A LIVIN
STRANGE TO

DATE: __ / __ / __

Describe your living room from a penguin's point of view.

_____

_____

_____

_____

_____

_____

_____

_____

ERY STRANGE IN A LIVING
OOM LOOKS VERY
ENGUIN. ◀ **Richard and Florence Atwater,**
Mr. Popper's Penguins

DATE: __ / __ / __

Draw three things in your living room that a penguin would see
as obstacles.

WHAT DO GIRLS DO WHO HAVEN'T ANY MOTHERS TO HELP THEM THROUGH THEIR TROUBLES?

Louisa May Alcott, *Good Wives*

How my mother helped me through a trouble today:

_____

_____

_____

_____

_____

BEING A FATHER
IS QUITE A BOTHER,
BUT I LIKE IT, RATHER.

Ogden Nash, "Soliloquy in Circles," *Versus*

How my father and I had fun together today (though I was a bit of a bother):

_____

_____

_____

_____

_____

ANIMALS ARE SUCH AGREEABLE FRIENDS— THEY ASK NO QUESTIONS, THEY PASS NO CRITICISM.

George Eliot, *Scenes of Clerical Life*

How my pet was an agreeable friend today:

_____

_____

_____

_____

_____

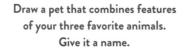

Draw a pet that combines features
of your three favorite animals.
Give it a name.

SWEETIE, WHEN LIFE PRESENTS CHALLENGES, YOU CAN BE EITHER A CHICKEN OR A CHAMPION. THE CHOICE IS YOURS!

Rachel Renée Russell, Dork Diaries: Tales from a Not-So-Fabulous Life

DATE: __ / __ / __

HOW I WAS A CHICKEN TODAY:

_____

_____

_____

_____

_____

DATE: __ / __ / __

HOW I WAS CHAMPION TODAY:

_____

_____

_____

_____

_____

I'M REALLY HAPPY TO BE ME, AND I'D LIKE TO THINK PEOPLE LIKE ME MORE BECAUSE I'M HAPPY WITH MYSELF.

Adele

I'm really happy with myself today because:

_____

_____

_____

_____

_____

A joy that's shared is a joy made double.

English proverb

I shared this joy with my friend today:

_____

_____

_____

_____

_____

DATE: __ / __ / __

IF I COULD HAVE A SUPERPOWER, THIS IS WHAT IT WOULD BE:

_____

_____

_____

_____

_____

_____

_____

_____

DATE: __/__/__

DRAW YOURSELF USING YOUR SUPERPOWER.

There's only one corner of the universe you can be certain of improving, and that's your own self.

Aldous Huxley

This is how I tried to improve myself today:

_____

_____

_____

_____

_____

A DETERMINED SOUL WILL DO
MORE WITH A RUSTY MONKEY
WRENCH THAN A LOAFER WILL
ACCOMPLISH WITH ALL THE TOOLS
IN A MACHINE SHOP.

Rupert Hughes

What I am determined to do:

_____

_____

_____

_____

_____

The simplest toy, one which even the youngest child can operate, is called a grandparent.

Sam Levenson

DATE: __ / __ / __

WHY I LIKE TO VISIT MY GRANDPARENTS:

_____

_____

_____

_____

_____

DATE: __ / __ / __

SOMETHING SPECIAL I GET TO DO ONLY WITH MY GRANDPARENTS:

_____

_____

_____

_____

_____

MISTRESS MARY ALWAYS FELT THAT HOWEVER MANY YEARS SHE LIVED SHE SHOULD NEVER FORGET THAT FIRST MORNING WHEN HER GARDEN BEGAN TO GROW.

Frances Hodgson Burnett, *The Secret Garden*

Here is a drawing of something I helped grow:

TO GET THE BEST RESULTS, YOU MUST TALK TO YOUR VEGETABLES.

Charles, Prince of Wales

A gardening trick I've learned:

_____

_____

_____

_____

_____

DATE: __/__/__

MY TOP 5 FOODS

Today I ate _____.

Never eat more than you can lift.

Miss Piggy

Today I ate my weight in _____.

Decorate this skateboard.

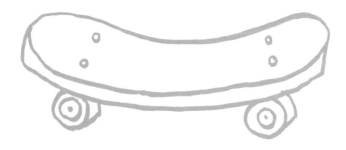

Decorate this bike helmet.

IT IS BEST TO WIN WITHOUT FIGHTING.

Sun Tzu, The Art of War

DATE: __/__/__

HOW I WON AT HOME WITHOUT FIGHTING TODAY:

_____

_____

_____

_____

_____

DATE: __/__/__

HOW I WON AT SCHOOL WITHOUT FIGHTING TODAY:

_____

_____

_____

_____

_____

DATE: ___/___/___

IT'S ALL THAT THE YOUNG CAN DO FOR THE OLD, TO SHOCK THEM AND KEEP THEM UP TO DATE.

George Bernard Shaw, *Fanny's First Play*

How I shocked my parents today:

_____

_____

_____

_____

_____

GIFTS MUST AFFECT THE RECEIVER TO THE POINT OF SHOCK.

Walter Benjamin

A shockingly great gift I received today:

_____

_____

_____

_____

_____

WRITE SOMETHING WEIRD

Write a story about a weird noise coming from a spooky house.

_____

_____

_____

_____

_____

_____

_____

_____

_____

DRAW SOMETHING WEIRD

Draw something that smells weird.

This smells like _____.

I've missed more than 9,000
shots in my career. I've lost
almost 300 games. . . .
I've failed over and over
and over again in my life.
And that is why I succeed.

Michael Jordan

After many failures, today I succeeded at:

_____

_____

_____

_____

_____

DATE: __ / __ / __

*I know of no genius
but the genius
of hard work.*

J. M. W. Turner

How I worked like a genius today:

_____

_____

_____

_____

JUDY MOODY

WAS IN A MOOD.

NOT A GOOD MOOD.

A *BAD* MOOD.

Megan McDonald, *Judy Moody*

DATE: __ / __ / __

WHAT PUT ME IN A BAD MOOD TODAY:

_____

_____

_____

_____

_____

DATE: __ / __ / __

WHAT PUT ME IN A GOOD MOOD TODAY:

_____

_____

_____

_____

_____

I LIKE BORING THINGS.

Andy Warhol

A lot of people might think these things are boring, but I like:

_____

_____

_____

_____

_____

LIFE'S TOO SHORT FOR CHESS.

Henry J. Byron

Today I played my favorite board game, _____.

DATE: __ / __ / __

RICHES ARE FOR SPENDING.

Francis Bacon

What I spent money on today:

_____

_____

_____

_____

_____

Tucker Mouse cleared his throat. . . .
[T]he Times Square subway
station. . . . [I]t was here that
I learned the value of economicness—
which means saving.

George Selden, *The Cricket in Times Square*

What I am saving up for:

_____

_____

_____

_____

_____

DATE: ___ / ___ / ___

*You have been
my friend. . . .
That in itself is
a tremendous thing.*

E. B. White, *Charlotte's Web*

The tremendous thing about my friendship with _____ is:

_____

_____

_____

_____

_____

DATE: __ / __ / __

TOKENS OF FRIENDSHIP

Today I:

○ shared this great song: _____

with: _____.

○ lent my favorite book: _____

to: _____.

○ shared this hysterical video: _____

with: _____.

○ made this yummy treat: _____

for: _____.

○ other: _____

with/to/for: _____.

ASK A TOAD WHAT
IS BEAUTY. . . .
HE WILL ANSWER
THAT IT IS THE FEMALE
WITH TWO GREAT ROUND
EYES COMING OUT OF
HER LITTLE HEAD,
HER LARGE FLAT MOUTH,
HER YELLOW BELLY
AND BROWN BACK.

Voltaire

ASK A HIPPOPOTAMUS WHAT BEAUTY IS, AND IT WILL ANSWER:

_____

_____

_____

_____

_____

DATE: __ / __ / __

ASK A SNAKE WHAT BEAUTY IS, AND IT WILL ANSWER:

_____

_____

_____

_____

_____

Being smart is cooler than anything in the world.

Michelle Obama

How I am cool today:

_____

_____

_____

_____

_____

_____

EUREKA!
[I'VE FOUND IT!]

Archimedes

Eureka! I've figured out _____.

I AM THE
GREATEST!

▲
Muhammad Ali
▼

I am the greatest at _____.

TRY TO BE LIKE THE TURTLE—AT EASE IN YOUR OWN SHELL.

Bill Copeland

Where I always feel comfortable:

_____

_____

_____

_____

_____

DATE: __ / __ / __

Lend a Hand

This is an issue I care about: _____

Today I wrote to: ◯ the president

◯ my senator

◯ my congressperson

◯ someone else: _____

DATE: __ / __ / __

Never doubt that a small
group of thoughtful,
committed citizens
can change the world.
In fact it's the only thing
that ever has.

Margaret Mead, attrib.

My friends and I organized to improve our community by:

_____

_____

_____

_____

_____

THE BEST THING FOR BEING SAD... IS TO LEARN SOMETHING.

T. H. White, *The Once and Future King*

It cheered me up to learn this:

_____

_____

_____

_____

_____

ALL OF US ARE WATCHERS—OF TELEVISION,
OF TIME CLOCKS, OF TRAFFIC ON THE
FREEWAY—BUT FEW ARE OBSERVERS.
EVERYONE IS LOOKING, NOT MANY
ARE SEEING.

Peter M. Leschak

What I observed today:

_____

_____

_____

_____

_____

MY TOP 5 PETS

1 _____

2 _____

3 _____

4 _____

5 _____

Today I got to play with a _____.

DATE: __ / __ / __

THE GREAT PLEASURE OF A DOG IS THAT YOU MAY MAKE A FOOL OF YOURSELF WITH HIM AND NOT ONLY WILL HE NOT SCOLD YOU, BUT HE WILL MAKE A FOOL OF HIMSELF TOO.

Samuel Butler

How an animal and I both made fools of ourselves today:

_____

_____

_____

_____

_____

IF THERE'S ONE THING I'VE LEARNE
CAN'T GIVE UP ON YOU
TEMPTING THE

DATE: __ / __ / __

Why I wanted to give up on my family today:

_____

_____

_____

_____

_____

_____

_____

VER THE EONS, IT'S THAT YOU
AMILY, NO MATTER HOW
AKE IT. ◀ **Rick Riordan,** *The Sea of Monsters*

DATE: __ / __ / __

Why I can't give up on my family:

_____

_____

_____

_____

_____

_____

_____

DATE: __ / __ / __

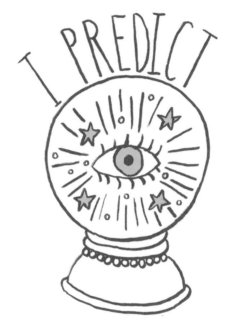

I predict that when I am in college, the hottest new technology will be:

_____

_____

_____

[IN THE FUTURE] THE INTERNET WILL DISAPPEAR.... [Y]OU WON'T EVEN SENSE IT. IT WILL BE PART OF YOUR PRESENCE ALL THE TIME.

Eric Schmidt

How I think the internet of the future will work:

_____

_____

_____

_____

_____

Make a drawing all in shades of the color you love the most.

Most Beautiful Color

Redo the drawing on the left in shades of the color you hate the most.

WHAT TO ONE MAN IS FOOD, TO ANOTHER IS RANK POISON.

Lucretius, *Lucretius on the Nature of Things*

DATE: __ / __ / __

NO ONE BELIEVES THAT I LIKE TO EAT:

_____

_____

_____

DATE: __ / __ / __

I CAN'T BELIEVE THAT MOST PEOPLE LIKE TO EAT:

_____

_____

_____

DATE: __ / __ / __

I SEE IT, I WANT IT . . .
I DREAM IT, I WORK HARD
I GRIND 'TIL I OWN IT . . .
I SLAY . . .

Beyoncé, "Formation," Lemonade

What I slayed today:

_____

_____

_____

_____

_____

DATE: __ / __ / __

YOU JUST CAN'T BEAT THE PERSON WHO NEVER GIVES UP.

Babe Ruth

My success today because I didn't give up:

_____

_____

_____

_____

_____

SEE THINGS

Turn these scissors into a face with a mustache, a balloon vendor, dancers, a chicken, or something else!

DIFFERENTLY

DATE: __ / __ / __

Turn this doodle into any kind of tool (real or imaginary). Label it.

"My name's Gloria Dump,"
she said. "Ain't that a terrible
last name? Dump?"
"My last name is Buloni," I said.
"Sometimes the kids at school
back home in Watley called me
'Lunch Meat.'"

Kate DiCamillo, *Because of Winn-Dixie*

What I ◯ like ◯ don't like about my last name:

_____

_____

_____

_____

_____

DATE: __ / __ / __

A NICKNAME IS THE HEAVIEST STONE THAT THE DEVIL CAN THROW AT [YOU].

William Hazlitt, "On Nicknames"

My nickname(s):

_____

_____

_____

_____

○ awesome ○ awful ○ meh

HE CAN'T THINK WITHOUT HIS HAT.

Samuel Beckett, *Waiting for Godot*

DATE: __ / __ / __

I CAN'T _____ WITHOUT MY _____.

DATE: __ / __ / __

HERE IS A PICTURE OF MY LUCKY _____:

I'M NOT AFRAID OF STORMS, FOR I'M LEARNING HOW TO SAIL MY SHIP.

Louisa May Alcott, *Little Women*

Today I wasn't afraid, even though _____.

The sun was rising behind her now; she could feel the heat on her back, and it gave her courage.

William Goldman, *The Princess Bride*

What gave me courage today:

_____

_____

_____

_____

_____

Draw your ideal classroom with people, real or imagined, including the teacher.

THERE IS MUCH PLEASURE TO BE GAINED FROM USELESS KNOWLEDGE.

Bertrand Russell

Something useless I learned at school today:

_____

_____

_____

_____

_____

Keep your eyes on the stars, but remember to keep your feet on the ground.

Theodore Roosevelt

DATE: __ / __ / __

THIS IS WHAT I DREAM OF:

_____

_____

_____

_____

_____

DATE: __ / __ / __

THIS IS HOW I AM PRACTICAL:

_____

_____

_____

_____

_____

IF I AM DOING NOTHING, I LIKE TO BE DOING NOTHING TO SOME PURPOSE.

Alan Bennett

My favorite thing to do when I am doing nothing:

_____

_____

_____

_____

_____

The time you enjoy wasting is not wasted time.

Laurence J. Peter

The person I enjoyed wasting time with today:

_____

_____

_____

_____

_____

DATE: __ / __ / __

IF I COULD LIVE AT ANY TIME IN THE PAST, THIS IS THE PERIOD I WOULD CHOOSE:

_____

_____

_____

_____

_____

_____

_____

DATE: __ / __ / __

DRAW YOURSELF IN THE CLOTHES OF YOUR FAVORITE TIME.

DON'T WORRY ABOUT MISTAKES. MAKING THINGS OUT OF MISTAKES, THAT'S CREATIVITY.

Peter Max

Something I created from a mistake today:

_____

_____

_____

_____

_____

UNTIL YOU'RE READY TO LOOK FOOLISH, YOU'LL NEVER HAVE THE POSSIBILITY OF BEING GREAT.

Cher

This is what happened today when I was ready to look foolish:

_____

_____

_____

_____

_____

TO KNOW
WHAT YOU KNOW
AND TO KNOW
WHAT YOU
DON'T KNOW—
THAT IS
KNOWLEDGE.

Confucius, *Analects*

DATE: __ / __ / __

WHAT I KNOW I KNOW:

_____

_____

_____

_____

_____

DATE: __ / __ / __

WHAT I KNOW I DON'T KNOW:

_____

_____

_____

_____

_____

Ron was seriously affronted when a
medieval wizard called out that he clearly
had a bad case of spattergroit. . . .
"I have not got spattergroit!"
"But the unsightly blemishes upon
your visage, young master—"
"They're freckles!" said Ron furiously.

J. K. Rowling, *Harry Potter and the Order of the Phoenix*

Draw a bad case of spattergroit.

The thing I love about freckles is that no two patterns are the same—they're specific to you and you alone.

Ralph Souffrant

My favorite pattern of freckles:

MY TOP 5 STORES

Today I shopped at _____.

The odds of going to the
store for a loaf of bread
and coming out with
only a loaf of bread
are three billion to one.

Erma Bombeck

What I couldn't resist buying at a store today:

_____

_____

_____

_____

Rearrange your room with what is already there.

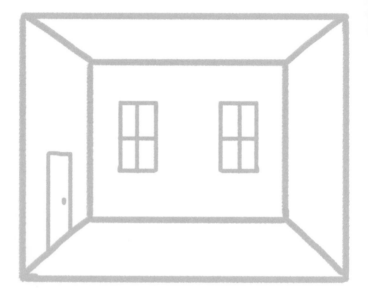

Redesign your room with your dream furniture.

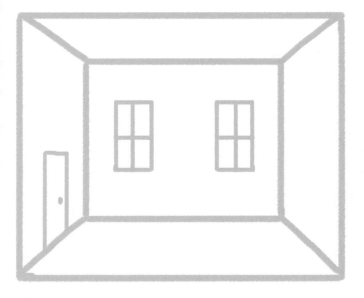

You can tell a lot about a fellow's character by his way of eating jellybeans.

Ronald Reagan

DATE: __ / __ / __

HOW I EAT JELLYBEANS:

_____

_____

WHAT THIS SAYS ABOUT ME:

_____

_____

DATE: __ / __ / __

HOW I EAT OREOS:

_____

_____

WHAT THIS SAYS ABOUT ME:

_____

_____

I LIKE COLORFUL TALES WITH BLACK BEGINNINGS AND STORMY MIDDLES AND CLOUDLESS BLUE-SKY ENDINGS. BUT ANY STORY WILL DO.

Katherine Applegate, *The One and Only Ivan*

The kind of tales I like these days:

_____

_____

_____

_____

_____

IN BOOKS I HAVE TRAVELED, NOT ONLY TO OTHER WORLDS, BUT INTO MY OWN.

Anna Quindlen, *How Reading Changed My Life*

In books, I have traveled:

- ⭕ the high seas
- ⭕ in outer space
- ⭕ to the time of dinosaurs
- ⭕ into the future
- ⭕ in haunted houses
- ⭕ in the bodies of animals
- ⭕ to imaginary castles
- ⭕ other: _____

WRITE SOMETHING WEIRD

Write about a weird dream you had.

_____

_____

_____

_____

_____

_____

_____

_____

_____

_____

DRAW SOMETHING WEIRD

Draw something from a weird dream you had.

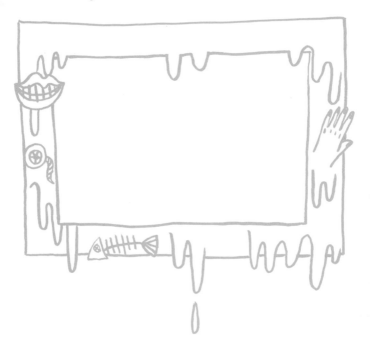

Write it on your heart that every day is the best day in the year.

Ralph Waldo Emerson

Why today was the best day in the year so far:

_____

_____

_____

_____

_____

DATE: __ / __ / __

STILL ROUND THE CORNER
THERE MAY WAIT
A NEW ROAD
OR A SECRET GATE.

J. R. R. Tolkien, *The Lord of the Rings*

A new road that I took today:

_____

_____

_____

_____

_____

THERE IS A
CHARM ABOUT
THE FORBIDDEN
THAT MAKES IT
UNSPEAKABLY
DESIRABLE.

Mark Twain, *Mark Twain's Notebook*

DATE: __ / __ / __

SOMETHING I AM FORBIDDEN TO DO THAT I REALLY WANT TO DO:

_____

_____

_____

_____

_____

DATE: __ / __ / __

SOMEWHERE I AM FORBIDDEN TO GO WHERE I REALLY WANT TO GO:

_____

_____

_____

_____

_____

I'M LOOKING FOR A DARE-TO-BE-GREAT SITUATION.

Lloyd Dobler, in Say Anything

Today I dared to be great:

_____

_____

_____

_____

_____

BE THE

NERD.

Mark Zuckerberg

This is how I was the nerd today:

_____

_____

_____

_____

_____

I was not the sort of boy who could train a dragon with the mere lifting of an eyebrow. I was not a natural at the Heroism business. I had to work at it.

Cressida Cowell, *How to Train Your Dragon*

How I worked at being a hero today:

_____

_____

_____

_____

_____

It's all to do with the training: you can do a lot if you're properly trained.

Queen Elizabeth II

How my training in _____ helped me today:

_____

_____

_____

_____

_____

I'VE NEVER HAD A HUMBLE OPINION. IF YOU'VE GOT AN OPINION, WHY BE HUMBLE ABOUT IT?

Joan Baez

IMNSHO (In my NOT so humble opinion) school is:

_____

_____

_____

DATE: __ / __ / __

Write some of your opinions about the world on these posters.

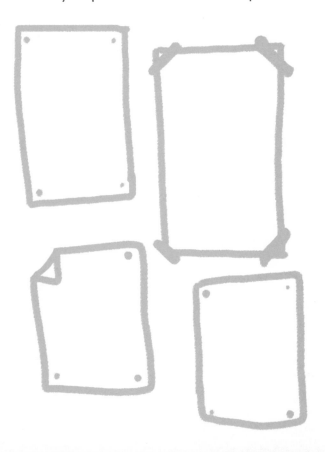

AT THE AGE OF SIX
I WANTED TO BE A COOK.
AT SEVEN I WANTED
TO BE NAPOLEON.
AND MY AMBITION HAS
BEEN GROWING STEADILY
EVER SINCE.

Salvador Dalí

DATE: __ / __ / __

AT THE AGE OF _____ I WANTED TO BE:

_____

_____

DATE: __ / __ / __

AT THE AGE OF _____ I WANTED TO BE:

_____

_____

DATE: __ / __ / __

RIGHT NOW I WANT TO BE:

_____

_____

DATE: __ / __ / __

Homework, I have discovered, involves a sharp pencil and thick books and long sighs.

Katherine Applegate, *The One and Only Ivan*

My homework involves:

_____

_____

_____

_____

_____

NO PEN, NO INK, NO TABLE, NO ROOM, NO TIME, NO QUIET, NO INCLINATION.

James Joyce

My excuse for not doing my homework today:

_____

_____

_____

_____

_____

DATE: __ / __ / __

MY FAVORITE COLORS ARE
THE COLORS OF THE SEA,
BLUE AND GRAY AND GREEN,
DEPENDING ON THE WEATHER.

Patricia MacLachlan, *Sarah, Plain and Tall*

My favorite colors are the colors of _____.

They are:

_____

_____

_____

COLORS, LIKE FEATURES, FOLLOW THE CHANGES OF THE EMOTIONS.

Pablo Picasso

The colors of my emotions today:

Morning   Afternoon   Night

Lend a Hand

Help out at an animal shelter.

○ Did it today!

HAPPINESS IS A WARM PUPPY.

Charles M. Schulz, *Happiness Is a Warm Puppy*

What I like about baby animals:

_____

_____

_____

_____

CHAMPIONS KEEP PLAYING UNTIL THEY GET IT RIGHT.

Billie Jean King

I kept working on this until I got it right today:

_____

_____

_____

_____

_____

DATE: __ / __ / __

Be like a postage stamp—stick to one thing till you get there.

Josh Billings

I stuck to this thing today (and I got there):

_____

_____

_____

_____

_____

MY TOP 5 CREATIVE ACTIVITIES

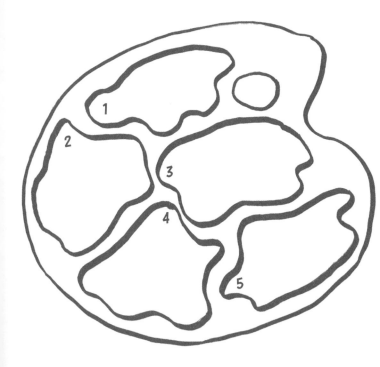

Today I created _____.

DATE: __ / __ / __

TO INVENT, YOU NEED A GOOD IMAGINATION AND A PILE OF JUNK.

Thomas Edison

What I did with my imagination and a pile of junk today:

_____

_____

_____

_____

A PERSON WHO HAS GOOD THOUGHT
GOOD THOUGHTS THEY WILL SHIN
AND YOU WILL ALWAY

DATE: __ / __ / __

Me having good thoughts:

CANNOT EVER BE UGLY. . . . [I]F YOU HAVE
OUT OF YOUR FACE LIKE SUNBEAMS
OOK LOVELY. ◀ **Roald Dahl**, *The Twits*

DATE: __ / __ / __

Me having bad thoughts:

DATE: __ / __ / __

I predict that when I grow up, the most popular food will be:

_____

_____

_____

Artichokes . . . are just plain annoying. . . . After all the trouble you go to, you get about as much actual "food" out of eating an artichoke as you would from licking thirty or forty postage stamps.

Miss Piggy

An annoying food I ate today:

_____

_____

Add meaningful charms to this bracelet for yourself or your friend.

DATE: __ / __ / __

Add a name and meaningful charms to this dog tag necklace for yourself or your friend.

I TRUST YOU TO
FIND THE GOOD
IN ME, BUT THE
BAD I MUST BE
SURE YOU DON'T
OVERLOOK.

Gail Carson Levine, *Ella Enchanted*

DATE: __/__/__

SOMETHING GOOD YOU WILL FIND IN ME TODAY:

_____

_____

_____

_____

DATE: __/__/__

THE BAD IN ME TODAY:

_____

_____

_____

_____

The problem is not the
problem. The problem
is your attitude
about the problem.

Ann Brashares, *The Sisterhood of the Traveling Pants*

What happened when I changed my attitude about my problem
today:

_____

_____

_____

_____

_____

DATE: __/__/__

IF PEOPLE EXPECT YOU TO BE BRAVE, SOMETIMES YOU PRETEND THAT YOU ARE, EVEN WHEN YOU ARE FRIGHTENED DOWN TO YOUR VERY BONES.

Sharon Creech, *Walk Two Moons*

What happened when I pretended to be brave today:

_____

_____

_____

_____

_____

SEE THINGS

Turn these pen caps into an airplane, a tall cap, an animal head, a mountain, Pinocchio lying down, or something else!

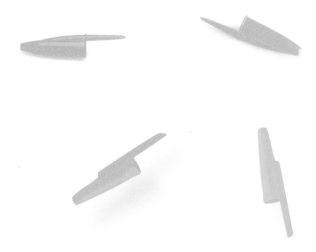

DIFFERENTLY

DATE: __ / __ / __

Turn this doodle into a house (real or imaginary). Label it.

PERSONALITY IS THE GLITTER
THAT SENDS YOUR LITTLE GLEAM
ACROSS THE FOOTLIGHTS AND THE
ORCHESTRA PIT INTO THAT BIG BLACK
SPACE WHERE THE AUDIENCE IS.

Mae West

When my personality glittered today:

_____

_____

_____

_____

_____

DATE: __/__/__

A LITTLE GLITTER CAN TURN YOUR WHOLE DAY AROUND.

▲
▼

Barbara Park, *Junie B., First Grader: Shipwrecked*

How glitter turned today around:

_____

_____

_____

_____

_____

If you want
to feel rich, just
count all the
things money
can't buy.

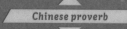
Chinese proverb

DATE: __ / __ / __

THINGS I TREASURE THAT MONEY CAN'T BUY:

_____

_____

_____

DATE: __ / __ / __

SPECIAL GIFTS I GAVE THAT MONEY CAN'T BUY:

_____

_____

_____

The sight of the stars always makes me dream.

Vincent van Gogh

My starry dream last night:

_____

_____

_____

_____

_____

DATE: __ / __ / __

YOU MUST NOT BLAME
ME IF I DO TALK
TO THE CLOUDS.

Henry David Thoreau

My cloudy conversation today:

_____

_____

_____

_____

_____

Everyone likes birds.
What wild creature is
more accessible to our
eyes and ears?

David Attenborough

Draw a beautiful bird you saw and heard today.

Turn these thumbprints into colorful birds.

CHAMPIONS AREN'T MADE IN GYMS. . . . [T]HEY HAVE TO HAVE THE SKILL AND THE WILL. BUT THE WILL MUST BE STRONGER THAN THE SKILL.

Muhammad Ali

DATE: __ / __ / __

HOW I USED MY SKILL TODAY:

_____

_____

_____

_____

_____

DATE: __ / __ / __

HOW I USED MY WILL TODAY:

_____

_____

_____

_____

_____

DATE: __/__/__

SOME BOOKS ARE TO BE TASTED, OTHERS TO BE SWALLOWED, AND SOME FEW TO BE CHEWED AND DIGESTED.

Francis Bacon, "Of Studies"

Book to be tasted:

_____

_____

Book to be swallowed:

_____

_____

Book to be chewed and digested:

_____

_____

SOME DAY
YOU WILL BE
OLD ENOUGH TO
START READING
FAIRY TALES AGAIN.

C. S. Lewis, *The Lion, the Witch, and the Wardrobe*

A fairy tale I read again today:

_____

_____

DATE: __ / __ / __

IF I WERE PRESIDENT OF THE UNITED STATES, THIS IS WHAT I WOULD DO RIGHT NOW:

_____

_____

_____

_____

_____

_____

_____

DATE: __ / __ / __

DRAW YOUR PICTURE ON THIS DOLLAR BILL.

DATE: __ / __ / __

GO DIRECTLY—SEE
WHAT SHE'S DOING, AND
TELL HER SHE MUSTN'T.

Punch magazine

When my parents blamed me unfairly today:

_____

_____

_____

_____

_____

*It is not a bad thing
that children should
occasionally, and politely,
put parents in their place.*

Colette, "The Priest on the Wall," *My Mother's House*

How I politely put my parents in their place today:

_____

_____

_____

_____

_____

VISITS ALWAYS GIVE PLEASURE— IF NOT THE ARRIVAL, THE DEPARTURE.

Portuguese proverb

DATE: __/__/__

OMG! I'M GLAD _____ VISITED TODAY.

DATE: __/__/__

OMG! I'M GLAD _____ FINALLY LEFT TODAY.

DATE: __ / __ / __

WHAT'S WRONG WITH BEING
NORMAL, FOR THOR'S SAKE?
WHAT'S WRONG WITH JUST BEING
SO-SO AT STUFF?

Cressida Cowell, *How to Steal a Dragon's Sword*

Why I was happy to be just normal today:

_____

_____

_____

_____

_____

IF YOU ARE ALWAYS TRYING TO BE NORMAL, YOU WILL NEVER KNOW HOW AMAZING YOU CAN BE.

Maya Angelou

How I tried to be amazing today:

_____

_____

_____

_____

_____

MY TOP 5 CLASSES AT SCHOOL

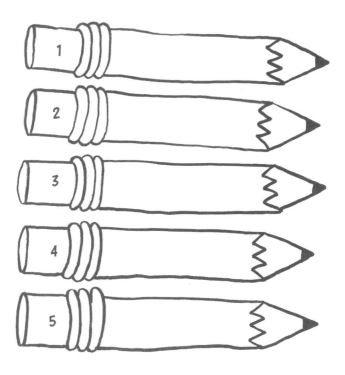

1

2

3

4

5

The best part of school today was _____.

If you want to know the reason why I'm standing here, it's because of education. I never cut class.

Michelle Obama

Where I want to be standing at the end of my education:

_____

_____

_____

_____

DATE: __ / __ / __

Create a comic strip of something you did today. Draw cartoons in these four boxes.

DATE: __ / __ / __

Add speech bubbles to your comic strip.

It made her think that it was curious how much nicer a person looked when he smiled.

Frances Hodgson Burnett, *The Secret Garden*

DATE: __ / __ / __

ME SMILING:

DATE: __ / __ / __

ME NOT SMILING:

IT IS THE BEST OF ALL TRADES, TO MAKE SONGS, AND THE SECOND BEST TO SING THEM.

Hilaire Belloc, "On Song"

Where I like to make music:

◯ in the shower/bath

◯ on the bus

◯ in math class

◯ at the dinner table

◯ other: _____

YOU JUST PICK A CHORD, GO TWANG, AND YOU'VE GOT MUSIC.

Sid Vicious

How I make music:

_____

_____

_____

_____

_____

WRITE SOMETHING WEIRD

Write a review of a weird meal.

_____

_____

_____

_____

_____

_____

_____

_____

_____

_____

DRAW SOMETHING WEIRD

Fill this plate with a weird dinner.

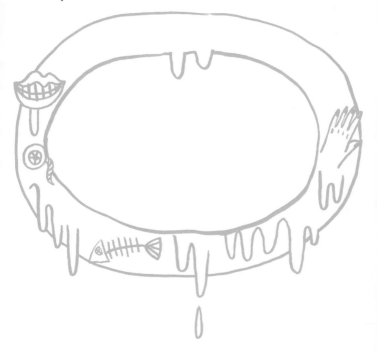

DATE: __/__/__

Spring is nature's way of saying, "Let's party!"

Robin Williams

How I partied in the spring weather today:

_____

_____

_____

_____

_____

DATE: __ / __ / __

LET THE WILD RUMPUS START!

Maurice Sendak, Where the Wild Things Are

Best. Party. Ever:

_____

_____

_____

_____

_____

NOBODY WINS UNLESS EVERYBODY WINS.

Bruce Springsteen

DATE: __ / __ / __

HERE'S HOW WE ALL WON TODAY:

_____

_____

_____

_____

_____

DATE: __ / __ / __

THESE ARE THE PEOPLE ON OUR WINNING TEAM:

_____

_____

_____

_____

_____

OCCASIONALLY INDULGING IN A DO-NOTHING DAY IS MORE THAN WORTH THE PRICE.

Malcolm Forbes

What happened on this do-nothing day—priceless!

_____

_____

_____

_____

_____

ABEL ALSO KEPT BUSY TAKING IT EASY. ONLY WHEN TAKING IT EASY, HE'D LEARNED, COULD ONE PROPERLY DO ONE'S WONDERING.

William Steig, *Abel's Island*

What I wondered while taking it easy today:

_____

_____

_____

_____

_____

DATE: __ / __ / __

We never forgive those who make us blush.

Jean-François de La Harpe, *Mélanie*

_____ made me blush today

by _____

_____.

ONE OF THE MOST TIME-CONSUMING THINGS IS TO HAVE AN ENEMY.

E. B. White

How I turned my enemy into a friend today:

_____

_____

_____

_____

_____

DATE: __ / __ / __

Summer afternoon—
summer afternoon . . .
the two most beautiful
words in the English
language.

Henry James

My favorite part of summer:

_____

_____

_____

_____

_____

Draw someone with you on this beach blanket.

I KEPT ALWAYS
TWO BOOKS
IN MY POCKET,
ONE TO READ,
ONE TO
WRITE IN.

Robert Louis Stevenson

DATE: __ / __ / __

WHAT I READ TODAY:

_____

_____

_____

_____

_____

DATE: __ / __ / __

WHAT I WROTE TODAY:

_____

_____

_____

_____

_____

"If life is so bad, how come you're so happy?"
"Did I say bad? I said it was tough. Nothing to make you happy like doing good on a tough job, now is there?"

Katherine Paterson, *The Great Gilly Hopkins*

A tough job that made me happy today:

_____

_____

_____

_____

_____

THEY CAN DO ALL BECAUSE THEY THINK THEY CAN.

Virgil

What I think I can do today:

_____

_____

_____

_____

_____

*Isn't it nice to think
that tomorrow is
a new day with no
mistakes in it yet?*

L. M. Montgomery, *Anne of Green Gables*

Today's mistake I won't make tomorrow:

_____

_____

_____

_____

WHAT MIGHT SEEM TO BE A SERIES OF UNFORTUNATE EVENTS MAY, IN FACT, BE THE FIRST STEPS OF A JOURNEY.

Violet Baudelaire,
in *Lemony Snicket's A Series of Unfortunate Events*

An unfortunate event that became the first step in a journey today:

_____

_____

_____

_____

_____

DATE: __/__/__

Lend a Hand

Teach a younger child to:
- ⃝ ride a bike
- ⃝ do yo-yo tricks
- ⃝ juggle
- ⃝ do a card trick
- ⃝ play a board game
- ⃝ tame a dragon
- ⃝ something else: _____

⃝ **Did it today!**

THOSE WHO ARE HAPPIEST
ARE THOSE WHO DO
THE MOST FOR OTHERS.

Booker T. Washington

What I did for someone else today:

Remember well
and bear in mind
A constant friend
is hard to find.

Laura Ingalls Wilder, *Little House in the Ozarks*

How I made a new friend today:

_____

_____

_____

_____

_____

THE ONLY WAY TO HAVE A FRIEND IS TO BE ONE.

Ralph Waldo Emerson

How I was a good friend today:

_____

_____

_____

_____

_____

DATE: __ / __ / __

MY TOP 5 PLACES To TRAVEL

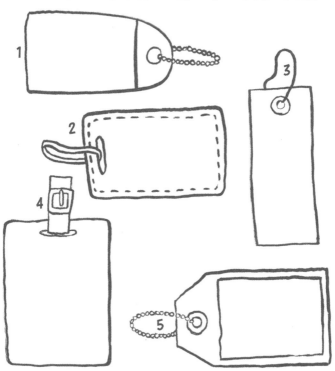

Today I went to _____.

THE BEST WAY OF TRAVEL, HOWEVER, IF YOU AREN'T IN ANY HURRY AT ALL, IF YOU DON'T CARE WHERE YOU ARE GOING, IF YOU DON'T LIKE TO USE YOUR LEGS,... IF YOU DON'T WANT TO BE ANNOYED AT ALL BY ANY CHOICE OF DIRECTIONS, IS IN A BALLOON.

William Pène du Bois, *The Twenty-One Balloons*

Today I traveled my favorite way: _____.

LEARN
BY
DOING.

Aristotle

DATE: __ / __ / __

HOW I LEARN BEST:

_____

_____

_____

_____

_____

DATE: __ / __ / __

SOMETHING I LEARNED BY DOING TODAY:

_____

_____

_____

_____

_____

I predict that when I grow up, the climate will be:

_____

_____

A LOT OF PEOPLE LIKE SNOW. I FIND IT TO BE AN UNNECESSARY FREEZING OF WATER.

Carl Reiner

A lot of people like _____.

I find it to be _____

_____.

DATE: __ / __ / __

Draw three product logos from memory here (for example, the symbol for Apple or McDonald's):

Now look at the original and give your version a grade

(A, B, C, D, F): _____

DATE: __ / __ / __

Draw the inside of your refrigerator from memory here:

Now check inside the fridge and give your memory a grade

(A, B, C, D, F): _____

How to be green?. . . Here's the answer. Consume less. Share more. Enjoy life.

Penny Kemp and Derek Wall,
A Green Manifesto for the 1990s

DATE: __ / __ / __

HOW I CONSUMED LESS TODAY:

_____

_____

_____

_____

_____

DATE: __ / __ / __

HOW I SHARED MORE TODAY:

_____

_____

_____

_____

_____

IN EVERY JOB THAT MUST BE DONE, THERE IS AN ELEMENT OF FUN. YOU FIND THE FUN AND— "SNAP!"—THE JOB'S A GAME.

Mary Poppins, in *Mary Poppins*

How—snap!—I turned a chore into a game today:

_____

_____

_____

_____

_____

DATE: __ / __ / __

It's good to play, and you must keep in practice.

Jerry Seinfeld

How I practiced playing today:

_____

_____

_____

_____

_____

SEE THINGS

DATE: __ / __ / __

Turn these bottle caps into a sun, a face, a button, a snowman, a soccer ball, or something else!

DIFFERENTLY

DATE: __/__/__

Turn this doodle into a flower (real or imaginary). Label it.

Believe me, my young friend, there is nothing—absolutely nothing—half so much worth doing as simply messing about in boats.

Kenneth Grahame, *The Wind in the Willows*

Why messing about in _____ was worth doing today:

_____

_____

NOT ALL THOSE WHO WANDER ARE LOST.

J. R. R. Tolkien, *The Fellowship of the Ring*

When I wandered today, I was actually _____

_____.

Oh, never mind the fashion. When one has a style of one's own, it is always twenty times better.

Margaret Oliphant, Miss Marjoribanks

DATE: __/__/__

SOMETHING FASHIONABLE THAT I WOULD NEVER WEAR:

_____

_____

_____

_____

_____

DATE: __/__/__

SOMETHING I WEAR THAT SHOWS MY OWN STYLE:

_____

_____

_____

_____

_____

DATE: __ / __ / __

EVERYTHING IS A MIRACLE. IT IS A MIRACLE THAT ONE DOES NOT DISSOLVE IN ONE'S BATH LIKE A LUMP OF SUGAR.

Pablo Picasso

Something miraculous that happened today:

_____

_____

_____

_____

_____

WATCH WITH GLITTERING EYES THE WHOLE WORLD AROUND YOU, BECAUSE THE GREATEST SECRETS ARE ALWAYS HIDDEN IN THE MOST UNLIKELY PLACES. THOSE WHO DON'T BELIEVE IN MAGIC WILL NEVER FIND IT.

Roald Dahl, *The Minpins*

Where I found magic today:

_____

_____

_____

_____

_____

I just say, "Never give up."...
[I]f you just push through the
struggles and the hard times,
it'll be so worth it in the end,
because you will be able to
get to your dreams.

Chloe Kim

This is my dream:

_____

_____

_____

_____

_____

DATE: __ / __ / __

Estimate then test how many reps you can do in 1 minute:

EXERCISE	ESTIMATES	ACTUAL
JUMPING JACKS		
PUSH-UPS		
BASKETS MADE		
DRIBBLES		
CARTWHEELS		
SOMERSAULTS		
YARDS RUN		

I RARELY DRAW WHAT
I FEEL IN

DATE: __ / __ / __

Draw what you SEE here:

I SEE—I DRAW WHAT MY BODY. ◀ Barbara Hepworth

DATE: __ / __ / __

Draw what you FEEL here:

DATE: __/__/__

THE SWEETEST
OF ALL SOUNDS
IS PRAISE.

Xenophon

The sweetest praise I heard today:

_____

_____

_____

_____

_____

A little praise Goes a great ways.

Ralph Waldo Emerson

I praised _____ for _____ today.

DATE: __ /__ /__

IF I COULD CHANGE ONE THING ABOUT MY LIFE, IT WOULD BE THIS:

_____

_____

_____

_____

_____

_____

_____

IF...

DATE: __ / __ / __

IF I COULD CHANGE ONE THING ABOUT THE WORLD, IT WOULD BE THIS:

_____

_____

_____

_____

_____

_____

_____

_____

"If seven maids, with seven mops,
Swept it for half a year,
Do you suppose," the Walrus said,
"That they could get it clear?"
"I doubt it," said the Carpenter,
And shed a bitter tear.

Lewis Carroll, *Through the Looking Glass*

An impossible cleaning chore today:

_____

_____

_____

_____

_____

NEATNESS WAS NOT ONE OF THE THINGS HE AIMED AT IN LIFE.

George Selden, *The Cricket in Times Square*

My aims in life:

○ neatness

○ messiness

○ other: _____

DATE: __ / __ / __

SOME CHANGES HAPPEN DEEP DOWN INSIDE OF YOU. AND THE TRUTH IS, ONLY YOU KNOW ABOUT THEM.

Judy Blume, *Tiger Eyes*

Some changes deep down inside me that only I know about:

_____

_____

_____

DATE: __ / __ / __

Do this page last (promise!).

This is how I rate my life today, after doing one fun thing every day:

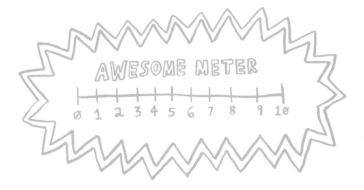

Now compare this to the Awesome Meter on page 3.

Published in the United States by Clarkson Potter/Publishers,
an imprint of the Crown Publishing Group, a division of
Penguin Random House LLC, New York.
crownpublishing.com
clarksonpotter.com

CLARKSON POTTER is a trademark and POTTER with colophon
is a registered trademark of Penguin Random House LLC.

ISBN 978-0-525-57541-2

Printed in China

Conceived and compiled by Dian G. Smith and Robie Rogge
Book design by Nicole Block
Cover design by Jessie Kaye
Illustrations by Christina Lee

10 9 8 7 6 5 4 3 2 1

First Edition